www.12StoryLibrary.com

12-Story Library is an imprint of Peterson Publishing Company and Press Room Editions.

Produced for 12-Story Library by Red Line Editorial

Photographs ©: Danny Moloshok/AP Images, cover, 1, 14; Frank Franklin II/AP Images, 4; John Shearer/Invision/AP Images, 5; Mark J. Terrill/AP Images, 6; Gerald Herbert/AP Images, 9; David J. Phillip/AP Images, 10; Michael Thomas/AP Images, 11; Oleksiy Naumov/ Shutterstock Images, 12, 13; Ringo H.W. Chiu/AP Images, 15; Greg Wahl-Stephens/AP Images, 16, 28; Wilfredo Lee/AP Images, 18; Lori Shepler/AP Images, 19, 29; Marcio Jose Sanchez/AP Images, 20; Seth Wenig/AP Images, 22; Charles Rex Arbogast/AP Images, 23; AP Images, 24; Debby Wong/Shutterstock Images, 26; Sue Ogrocki/AP Images, 27

ISBN
978-1-63235-021-3 (hardcover)
978-1-63235-081-7 (paperback)
978-1-62143-062-9 (hosted ebook)

Library of Congress Control Number: 2014946805

Printed in the United States of America
Mankato, MN
October, 2014

Go beyond the book. Get free, up-to-date content on this topic at 12StoryLibrary.com.

TABLE OF CONTENTS

CARMELO ANTHONY ONE OF THE NBA'S TOP SCORERS

Anthony shoots over Washington Wizards player Trevor Ariza in a 2014 game.

Carmelo Anthony moved to Baltimore, Maryland, when he was eight years old. Sports helped to keep him out of trouble when he was a child. He matured into a star player. As a junior in high school, the *Baltimore Sun* newspaper named Anthony the top high school player in the area. He was attending Towson Catholic at the time. He played at Oak Hill Academy in Virginia as a senior to help get ready for college.

Anthony lifted Syracuse University to the NCAA title in his freshman season. He was named the tournament's Most Outstanding Player. He decided he was ready for the NBA.

6

Number of 3-pointers Anthony made in his 62-point game.

Birth date: May 29, 1984

Birthplace: Brooklyn, New York

Height: 6 feet 8 (2.03 m)

Weight: 230 pounds (104 kg)

Teams: Denver Nuggets, 2003–11; New York Knicks, 2011–

Breakthrough Season: Led Nuggets in scoring as a 19-year-old rookie

Awards: ESPN Rise all-decade team for high school basketball in the 2000s, Olympic gold medalist in 2008 and 2012

Anthony accepts the clutch player of the year award at the Kid's Choice Sports Awards with his son, Kiyan, in 2014.

Anthony uses his size and speed to be one of the best scorers in basketball. His quick moves open up room for his jump shot. His height also helps free him for dunks or shots near the basket. Anthony is still looking for his first NBA championship. But he did help the Denver Nuggets reach the Western Conference Finals in 2009.

Anthony has set team scoring records in the NBA and for Team USA in the Olympics. In 2012, he scored 37 points against Nigeria in the Olympics. It was the most points ever scored by a US player in a single game. He set the New York Knicks' team record by scoring 62 points in one game. His average of 25.3 points per game ranked in the top five of active players at the end of the 2013–14 season.

STEPHEN CURRY
A DOUBLE THREAT

Curry leaps up for a shot against the Los Angeles Clippers during the 2014 playoffs.

272

Number of 3-pointers
Curry made in the
2012–13 season.

Birth date: March 14, 1988
Birthplace: Akron, Ohio
Height: 6 feet 3 (1.91 m)
Weight: 185 pounds
(84 kg)
Team: Golden State
Warriors, 2009–
Breakthrough Season:
Set NBA record by
making 272 3-point
shots in 2012–13
season
Awards: 2011 Joe
Dumars NBA
Sportsmanship Award,
NCAA Tournament
Midwest Regional Most
Outstanding Player as
a sophomore

Stephen Curry is famous for his long-range shot. He combines this skill with his other duties. Curry is a point guard. It is his job to get the ball to his teammates. Opponents have to choose. They can try to stop Curry from shooting, or they can try taking away his passing options.

Curry knows how to get away from defenders. This makes him

A FAMILY OF ALL-STARS

Curry has a smooth release on his jump shot. This may look familiar to some longtime NBA fans. Dell Curry, Stephen's father, was also an NBA star. He was also an outstanding shooter from long distances. Curry's athletic family includes his mom, Sonya, and sister, Sydel. Both women played college volleyball. Curry's brother, Seth, also played in the NBA.

a successful shooter. He doesn't need much space to shoot. Curry showed that at Davidson College. While playing for Davidson, he led the nation in total scoring twice. He also set an NCAA record for most 3-pointers made in one season.

Curry led the NBA in 3-pointers in both the 2012–13 and 2013–14 seasons. He averaged more than three 3-pointers per game in both seasons.

ANTHONY DAVIS PROTECTS THE RIM

Anthony Davis was a guard until he grew seven inches (18 cm) midway through high school. That growth spurt helped transform him into the dominant inside force he is today.

In his only season at the University of Kentucky, Davis was regarded as the best college player in the country. He helped Kentucky win the national title. He received six major awards as the best player in the country. He was also the Final Four Most Outstanding Player.

The New Orleans Hornets selected Davis with the first pick of the 2012 NBA Draft. He was named to the all-rookie team in his first NBA season. But he kept improving his scoring, rebounding, and shot-blocking numbers in his second year. Davis is one of basketball's most effective rebounders and scorers. He especially stands out on defense. At Kentucky, he led the nation in blocked shots. By his second year as a pro, he also led the NBA in blocked shots.

2.8

Number of shots per game that Davis blocked in 2013–14.

Birth Date: March 11, 1993
Birthplace: Chicago, Illinois
Team: New Orleans Hornets/Pelicans, 2012–
Height: 6 feet 10 (2.08 m)
Weight: 220 pounds (100 kg)
Breakthrough Season: Became an all-star in his second season, 2013–14
Awards: NCAA Final Four Most Outstanding Player in 2012

Davis blocks a shot against the Charlotte Bobcats in 2012.

TIM DUNCAN'S CALM STYLE LEADS SPURS

Tim Duncan got a late start in basketball. He was a promising swimmer until the ninth grade. That year a hurricane wiped out the only Olympic-sized pool on the island of Saint Croix.

Duncan defends a shot during a game against the Miami Heat in 2014.

3

Number of NBA Finals MVP awards Duncan has won.

Birth date: April 25, 1976

Birthplace: Christiansted, Saint Croix, US Virgin Islands

Height: 6 feet 11 (2.11 m)

Weight: 248 pounds (112 kg)

Team: San Antonio Spurs, 1997–

Breakthrough Season: Helped lead the Spurs to their first NBA title in his second season, 1998–99

Awards: 1997 College Basketball Player of the Year, NBA Most Valuable Player in 2002 and 2003

After that, Duncan switched to basketball. He quickly became a star, and has quietly built a long and successful basketball career. Duncan does not have the showy style that helped make other players famous. He simply plays well year after year.

Many college basketball stars leave college early to turn pro. Duncan was different. He stayed at Wake Forest University for a full four years. The National Association of Basketball Coaches named him Defensive Player of the Year three times. He was named national Player of the Year as a senior in 1996–97.

The San Antonio Spurs chose Duncan first in the 1997 NBA Draft. The Spurs won four NBA championships in Duncan's first 10 seasons. But they were not done. Duncan kept working. In 2014, the Spurs won a fifth NBA title.

Duncan's game reflects his personality. He plays both power forward and center for the Spurs. Duncan developed the moves to score in the post position, near the basket. He also showed he could make jump shots from farther away. He gained respect by working hard and becoming a reliable defender, rebounder, and team player.

Duncan holds the championship trophy and shows off five fingers, representing the five NBA titles he has helped the Spurs win.

KEVIN DURANT EARNS 2014 MVP AWARD

Kevin Durant got started in the game while growing up in Washington, DC. He has been a star player at every level. He was named All-Metro Player of the Year as a senior in high school. Then he was honored as the McDonald's All-American game's Most Valuable Player (MVP).

He was Player of the Year in college basketball in his only season at the University of Texas. Then he was off to the NBA.

The Seattle SuperSonics drafted Durant second overall in 2007. In his first season, he was the NBA's

Durant drives to the basket during the 2010 World Championship Final against Turkey.

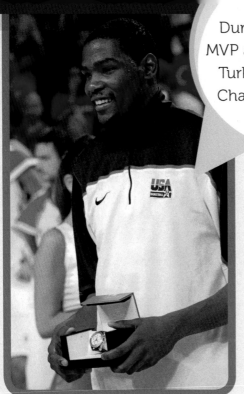

Durant was named MVP after helping beat Turkey in the World Championship Final in 2010.

the NBA MVP award while winning his fourth scoring title. He did this by setting up teammates and getting better at defense.

156

Number of points Durant scored in eight games in the 2012 Olympics.

Birth date: September 29, 1988

Birthplace: Suitland, Maryland

Height: 6 feet 9 (2.06 m)

Weight: 215 pounds (98 kg)

Teams: Seattle SuperSonics, 2007–08; Oklahoma City Thunder, 2008–

Breakthrough Season: Averaged 20.3 points per game as a 19-year-old rookie in 2007–08

Awards: 2007 College Basketball Player of the Year, 2008 NBA Rookie of the Year, 2014 NBA MVP

Rookie of the Year. Before the next season, the Seattle SuperSonics moved to Oklahoma City, Oklahoma. Here, they were renamed the Thunder. Durant led the team through the NBA ranks. The tall forward has moves that smaller NBA guards envy. He glides around the basketball court and scores from many angles.

Piling up points is nothing new for Durant. He led the NBA in scoring average for the fourth time in five seasons in 2013–14. His scoring is consistent. But Durant keeps improving in other areas. He earned

BLAKE GRIFFIN SLAMS DUNKS

Blake Griffin played baseball, football, and basketball as a child. In high school, he played alongside his older brother, Taylor. The Griffins made Oklahoma Christian School into a powerhouse. The team won four straight state championships. Blake was the state tournament MVP in Class 2A his final two years.

Griffin followed Taylor to the University of Oklahoma. After two standout seasons, Griffin was headed for the NBA. Griffin's NBA debut was delayed. But it was still spectacular. The Los Angeles Clippers chose Griffin with the first pick of the 2009 NBA Draft. He suffered a broken kneecap in the preseason. His injury kept him out the entire season. But when Griffin started his career a year later, in 2010, he won the NBA Rookie of the Year award.

Griffin is known for his dunking ability, as he shows here against the Sacramento Kings in 2014.

6

Number of consecutive Rookie of the Month awards Griffin won in 2010–11.

Birth date: March 16, 1989

Birthplace: Oklahoma City, Oklahoma

Height: 6 feet 10 (2.08 m)

Weight: 251 pounds (114 kg)

Team: Los Angeles Clippers, 2009–

Breakthrough Season: Led Clippers in scoring and rebounding as a rookie in 2010–11

Awards: 2009 College Basketball Player of the Year, 2011 NBA Rookie of the Year

Griffin's height and skill help him make shots over other players.

Griffin may be the league's most likely player to show up on ESPN's *SportsCenter* each night. His high-flying slam dunks show off his jumping ability. With Griffin dunking, rebounding, dribbling, and passing, the Clippers quickly improved. The team won its first Pacific Division championship during the 2012–13 season.

JAMES HARDEN RISES TO THE TOP

Oklahoma City Thunder selected James Harden third overall in the 2009 NBA Draft. Harden didn't start at first, but he still showed he could make a big impact on an NBA game. He then showed he could do even more from a spot in the starting five.

Harden started just two games during the 2011–12 season. But he still averaged 16.8 points per game

Harden (right) chases a loose ball during a game against the Portland Trail Blazers in 2014.

with the Thunder. When the season was over, Harden was selected Sixth Man of the Year in the NBA. He was considered the best player among those not on their team's starting five.

After beginning his pro career with the Thunder, Harden was traded to the Houston Rockets in 2012. They made Harden a starter. He averaged more than 25 points per game during his first two seasons in Houston. By the second season, he was regarded as one of the five best players in the entire league. He was named to the All-NBA first team for the 2013–14 season. Harden is easy to spot on the floor because of his distinctive thick beard. He also has a powerful build that helps him drive to the basket when he is not draining 3-point shots.

31.4

Number of minutes per game Harden played as the Thunder's sixth man in 2011–12.

Birth date: August 26, 1989

Birthplace: Los Angeles, California

Height: 6 feet 5 (1.95 m)

Weight: 220 pounds (100 kg)

Teams: Oklahoma City Thunder, 2009–12; Houston Rockets, 2012–

Breakthrough Season: Helped the Thunder reach the Western Conference Finals in 2010–11

Awards: Named NBA Sixth Man of the Year in 2012, All-NBA first team in 2014

OVERCOMING ASTHMA

Harden showed promise on the basketball court from a young age. First he had to get his asthma under control. Once he did, Harden became a high school starter as a sophomore. He later led his team to two state championships.

LeBRON JAMES REJOINS THE CAVALIERS

Fame came early for LeBron James. He was on the cover of *Sports Illustrated* as a junior in high school. The magazine predicted he would be an NBA superstar. James was drafted straight out of high school by the Cleveland Cavaliers in 2003. He quickly proved that he was worthy of the prediction. He led the Cavaliers to the NBA finals in 2007.

James had a decision to make in 2010. After seven years in the NBA, his contract was over. He could choose which team to play for next. The decision worked out well for James. He moved to the Miami Heat. There, he joined All-Star guard Dwyane Wade. Chris Bosh, another All-Star free agent, made the same decision that week in 2010. The three formed the base of a championship team. James and the Heat reached the next four NBA finals. James led the team to championships in 2012 and 2013.

James races toward the basket as a member of the Miami Heat in 2014.

In 2014, James returned to play with the Cavaliers.

James can do it all on the basketball court. He has strength and mobility. James can play and defend against every position. His skills include scoring, passing, rebounding, and defending.

THE DECISION

James announced his plans to play for the Heat on a television show. It was called *The Decision*. The show helped raise millions of dollars for charity. But some people did not like the show. The move was unpopular in Ohio, where James left behind his hometown team, the Cleveland Cavaliers.

James played with the Cavaliers from 2003 to 2010 and rejoined the team in 2014.

30.0
Number of points per game James scored when he won the NBA scoring title in 2007–08.

Birth date: December 30, 1984

Birthplace: Akron, Ohio

Height: 6 feet 8 (2.03 m)

Weight: 240 pounds (109 kg)

Teams: Cleveland Cavaliers, 2003–10, 2014–; Miami Heat, 2010–14

Breakthrough Season: Led Cleveland Cavaliers to 2007 NBA Finals

Awards: National high school Player of the Year in 2002 and 2003; 2004 NBA Rookie of the Year, Olympic gold medalist in 2008 and 2012, NBA MVP in 2009, 2010, 2012, and 2013; *Sports Illustrated* 2013 Sportsman of the Year

KEVIN LOVE IS DOUBLE TROUBLE

Kevin Love learned the game from his father, Stan. Stan was once an NBA player. Kevin moved from California to Oregon as a boy. He became Oregon's record-holder for points with 2,628. He helped lead Lake Oswego High School to three straight state championship games.

After one year at the University of California, Los Angeles, and a trip to college basketball's Final Four, Love was ready for the NBA. He was picked fifth overall by the Memphis Grizzlies in the 2008 NBA Draft. But he was traded that night to Minnesota. There, Love began his career.

Love is one of the strongest inside players in the NBA.

Love is double trouble for NBA teams. During his career with the Minnesota Timberwolves, Love has made the double-double seem routine. He regularly finishes games in double figures—10 or higher—in both points and rebounds. In the 2010–11 season, Love reached double figures in both points and rebounds in 53 straight games. This was the longest such streak in the NBA in 37 years. Love uses strength and hard work to get in position. He rebounds missed shots. He has also developed into one of the league's best scorers among big men. In 2014, Love was traded to the Cleveland Cavaliers, where he joined Olympic teammate LeBron James.

15.2

Number of rebounds per game Love had when he led the NBA in 2010–11.

Birth date: September 7, 1988

Birthplace: Santa Monica, California

Height: 6 feet 10 (2.08 m)

Weight: 260 pounds (118 kg)

Teams: Minnesota Timberwolves, 2008–14 Cleveland Cavaliers, 2014–

Breakthrough Season: Led the NBA in rebounding and became an All-Star in 2010–11

Awards: Most Improved Player during the 2010–11 season, 2012 Olympic gold medalist

CELEBRITY FAMILY

Love comes from a famous family. His father, Stan, played in the NBA for the Baltimore Bullets and Los Angeles Lakers in the early 1970s. Kevin's uncle, Mike Love, was a member of the popular band the Beach Boys. The Beach Boys rose to fame in the 1960s. They made it into the Rock and Roll Hall of Fame in 1988.

JOAKIM NOAH BRINGS THE DEFENSE

Joakim Noah lived in Paris, France, for much of his childhood. At age 13, he moved back to his birthplace of New York City. After high school, he played at the University of Florida. He helped lead the Gators to back-to-back national championships. Then the Chicago Bulls picked him ninth overall in the 2007 NBA Draft.

Noah is one of the NBA's hardest working players. He was named the best defensive player in the NBA for the 2013–14 season. It takes dedication and hard work to be the best on defense.

The center can score when needed. But he uses his skills everywhere on the

Noah (13) knocks the ball away from Cole Aldrich of the New York Knicks in 2014.

4

Number of years Noah averaged a double-double per game through his first seven NBA seasons.

Birth date: February 25, 1985

Birthplace: New York, New York

Height: 6 feet 11 (2.11 m)

Weight: 232 pounds (105 kg)

Team: Chicago Bulls, 2007–

Breakthrough Season: Averaged double digits in both points and rebounds for the first time in 2009–10

Awards: Most Outstanding Player of the Final Four in 2006, Defensive Player of the Year in 2013–14 season

WORLDLY PLAYER

Noah is a citizen of three countries. He was born in the United States. But his parents are from France and Sweden. This makes him a citizen of all three countries. Noah's father, Yannick Noah, was once a tennis champion. His mother, Cecilia Rodhe, also gained fame. She was named Miss Sweden in 1978.

court. Noah grabs rebounds and stops opponents from scoring. He is better than most big men when it comes to handling and passing the basketball.

Noah (left) accepts the Defensive Player of the Year award in 2014.

11

CHRIS PAUL RUNS THE SHOW FOR THE CLIPPERS

Paul directs his teammates while playing the Oklahoma City Thunder in 2014.

Chris Paul starred in basketball at West Forsyth High School in Clemmons, North Carolina. Paul then led Wake Forest University to the top of the national rankings for the first time ever.

Following two seasons at Wake Forest, Paul was ready for the NBA. The New Orleans Hornets picked him fourth overall in the 2005 NBA Draft. Paul quickly developed into one of the best point guards in the game. He won two Olympic gold medals, starting at the position for Team USA at the 2012 Games. Paul teamed with Blake Griffin to lead the Los Angeles Clippers to their first division title in 2012–13.

When the Clippers have the ball, it is often in Paul's hands. He plays point guard, running his team's offense. The point guard starts most plays. From there, Paul breaks down defenses. He can score. But more often, Paul sets up teammates. He draws the defense's attention. This leaves room for other players to score. Paul led the NBA in assists per game in his third and fourth NBA seasons.

3
Paul's uniform number and the reason he is nicknamed "CP3."

Birth date: May 6, 1985
Birthplace: Lewisville, North Carolina
Height: 6 feet 0 (1.83 m)
Weight: 175 pounds (79 kg)
Teams: New Orleans Hornets, 2005–2011; Los Angeles Clippers, 2011–
Breakthrough Season: Led the NBA in total steals in his rookie year of 2005–06
Awards: NBA Rookie of the Year in 2006, Olympic gold medalist in 2008 and 2012, All-NBA first team in 2008, 2012, 2013, and 2014

Paul applies constant pressure on opponents. Playing at high speed, Paul is a threat. He is known for taking the ball away from opponents. He led the NBA in steals six times in seven years. Paul was selected to the NBA All-Defensive team four times in that stretch.

RUSSELL WESTBROOK LEADS THUNDER'S PLAYOFF PUSH

Russell Westbrook grew up in California. He did not start on his high school basketball team until his junior year. One year later, one of the nation's most prestigious college programs offered him a scholarship. Westbrook played two seasons for the University of California, Los Angeles. He played in college basketball's Final Four both times. In 2008, he was drafted fourth overall by the Seattle SuperSonics. Just after that, the team moved to Oklahoma City to become the Thunder.

Westbrook (right) defends against Joe Johnson of the Brooklyn Nets in 2012.

Westbrook steals the ball and breaks away from the Spurs' Danny Green in 2014.

Along with Kevin Durant, Westbrook turned the Thunder into contenders. Westbrook attacks from his point guard position. He gets the ball to his teammates. He also goes hard to the basket. In his second pro season, and his first as a starter, the Thunder more than doubled their win total. Before long, they were battling the San Antonio Spurs for the honor of top team in the Western Conference. Westbrook took on the responsibility to score in the playoffs. Through the Thunder's first five playoff appearances, Westbrook averaged 24.1 points in 64 games.

26.7

Westbrook's playoff scoring average in 2014.

Birth date: November 12, 1988

Birthplace: Long Beach, California

Height: 6 feet 3 (1.91 m)

Weight: 187 pounds (85 kg)

Team: Oklahoma City Thunder, 2008–

Breakthrough Season: Led Thunder in assists as a rookie in 2008–09

Awards: 2012 Olympic gold medalist

FACT SHEET

- Basketball was invented in the late 1800s. Dr. James Naismith, a physical education teacher in Springfield, Massachusetts, developed the first set of rules in 1891. At first, players shot at peach baskets posted at the ends of the court. The game stopped with every successful shot because somebody had to climb a ladder and get the ball out of the peach basket. Eventually the bottoms were cut out of the baskets to speed up the game. Club teams formed at local YMCAs. In 1893, Vanderbilt University in Nashville, Tennessee, became the first college with its own basketball team.

- In the late 1940s, the United States had two professional basketball leagues. By 1949, the National Basketball League and the Basketball Association of America merged to form the NBA. The league grew and changed over the years. The most dramatic change came in the mid-1970s when the rival American Basketball Association (ABA) ran out of money. The NBA took in four new teams—the San Antonio Spurs, Denver Nuggets, Indiana Pacers, and New York (now Brooklyn) Nets—as the ABA folded.

- The National Basketball Association is made up of 30 teams. Those teams are split into the Eastern Conference and Western Conference. Both conferences have three divisions of five teams each. The top eight teams in each conference advance to playoffs to determine the league champion.

- Following each season, NBA teams select available amateur players from American colleges and other countries. Teams take turns picking players. Teams that miss the playoffs have a chance to pick first. A lottery system determines their exact order. Generally, the better a team does, the longer it has to wait to pick. The order can also change because teams trade their picks for players or other picks.

GLOSSARY

assist
A pass that leads to a basket by a teammate.

contract
A written agreement committing a player to a team. It also specifies how much the player is paid.

defense
The team trying to stop the other team from scoring.

NBA Draft
A process in which amateur players are selected and placed on NBA teams.

offense
The team that has control of the ball and tries to score.

playoffs
Games at the end of the season that decide a champion. When a team loses a playoff series, their season is over.

rebound
To retrieve a ball after a missed shot.

rookie
A professional player in his first year.

steal
Taking the ball away from an opposing player or team.

FOR MORE INFORMATION

Books

Frisch, Aaron. *Miami Heat*. Mankato, MN: Creative Paperbacks, 2012.

Rausch, David. *National Basketball Association*. Minneapolis: Bellwether Media, 2014.

Smallwood, John N. *Megastars 2011*. New York: Scholastic, 2011.

Websites

Basketball Reference
www.basketball-reference.com

ESPN
www.espn.com

National Basketball Association
www.nba.com

INDEX

About the Author

Tom Robinson is the author of more than three dozen books for children. He has written biographies and books about sports, history, and social issues. He lives in Clarks Summit, Pa.

READ MORE FROM 12-STORY LIBRARY

Every 12-Story Library book is available in many formats, including Amazon Kindle and Apple iBooks. For more information, visit your device's store or 12StoryLibrary.com.